GOLF

Other titles by Danny :-

Danny Gets to Grips with **Gardening**

Danny Gets to Grips with the **Motor Car**

Danny Gets to Grips with **Horse & Pony Care**

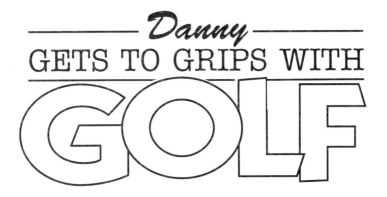

Danny
GETS TO GRIPS WITH
GOLF

DC Publishing Paperback

First Edition
Published in Great Britain 1995
by DC Publishing
11 Bryanston Village
Blandford Forum
Dorset DT11 0PR

Made and printed in Great Britain

For Tony & Ken

and all other Golfers who go to great lengths
to hit a little ball into a small black hole....
having achieved this in one stroke, they
walk around in disbelief and
talk about it for years.

CONTENTS

FOREWORD

" Being artistically inclined I appreciate the skill of Danny for, not only has he succeeded in producing characters and situations that actually exist and take place, I almost feel that I can recognise some of the Club members I have spent my life with. His ability to hide accurate detail within the humour of the cartoon makes each worthy of 'another look' - again and again!

They say that making people laugh is a special gift, to have the talent to do so with a pen and a brush is more than that, particularly when the content is directed at sportsmen who are critically possessive. Danny has these gifts and, as golfers say,

"He has won this match out in the country!" "

**Managing Director of
Woburn Golf and Country Club
and Member of the
B.B.C. Golf Commentary Team.**

The door is always open to anyone who
wants to take up golf....

11

But beware, it's easy to fall head over heels
in love with the game.

Today, more and more youngsters are
encouraged to play.

One great attraction of the game is that
golfers of various skills and abilities can meet
for a friendly match.

EQUIPMENT

Before rushing out and spending vast
amounts of money on kitting yourself out, go
to seek the advice of the club professional

Firstly, however, be sure he is professional.

If possible, before buying new clubs, try
them out......Remember, patience is the key.

Feeling comfortable with your clubs is
probably more important than anything else.

Get yourself a golf bag to suit your
carrying ability.

Don't forget, when it comes to playing in
Britain, waterproofs are a must.

It's advisable to carry an umbrella for those
passing showers.

To keep the grips in perfect condition, it is
best to wash them in hot soapy water....

Don't dry them too near a radiator.

Don't leave them unattended for too long!

When purchasing a pair of golfing shoes, buy
the best that you can afford.

STARTING TO PLAY

The best advice is to seek out the the club
professional for tuition right from the start.

To get the best results from your game first
and foremost WARM UP.
To loosen those muscles, try taking a bath.

It's a great way to relax and to concentrate
your mind on the game ahead,

but do be careful...you may get too relaxed!

It is inadvisable to play golf during a
thunderstorm.

Remember to keep an eye open for your
partner's ball.

Driving ranges offer a great opportunity for
practice and have the advantage that you
can stay as long as you like.

but never, ever attempt to pick up your balls!

Putting is an exact science.

GOLFING ETIQUETTE

From the moment you tee off it is important
to show courtesy.

Don't hit the ball until you are sure the
way ahead is clear.

A ball is declared lost if it hasn't been found within 5 minutes. Another ball should be selected and put into play.

All footprints, humps and holes in bunkers
should be smoothed out.

Keep quiet when others are playing their shots.

All divots must be replaced.

Never take your trolley on to the green.

When you have finished putting, replace the
flag swiftly and get off the green.

Never wear spiked shoes in the clubhouse.

Always wear the correct dress
in the golf club.

GOLFING HOLIDAYS

To progress more quickly, try taking a
specially designed holiday to improve
your game.

Chipping on the beach is great practice for
all those uneven surfaces.

A good holiday sharpens your reflexes

and will definitely improve your swing.....

You'll soon benefit from the knock on effect,

but be careful not to over indulge in
the local cuisine.

At the end of your golfing holiday, you are
sure to arrive home rested, relaxed and
eager to get back to the game.

10 TIPS TO ENHANCE YOUR GAME

Always arrive at the course in good time.

You will feel good when dressed well and
comfortably turned out.

If you have the money, get yourself
video-taped.......Mistakes are more
easily recognised

and you can invite your friends to
see you on the TV.

It's a good idea to check your stance &
alignment in a mirror.

Get acquainted with the rules.

If the weather is really bad, there may be no
alternative but to practise indoors.

One good way to develop a slow, rhythmic
swing is to use a broom or brush.

If you are not allowed on the course,
practise in the garden.

Find some good bedtime reading...
there are plenty of books on the market.

Jot down any useful tips you come across.

GOLFING
EXPRESSIONS

Three off the Tee.

Playing Through.

The Bunker Shot

A ball that is on a downward slope making
the player overstretch to take the intending
shot is called a **Hanging Lie**

A Fast Green.......

A Slow Green.

Commonly known as **Pin High**.

Out of Bounds

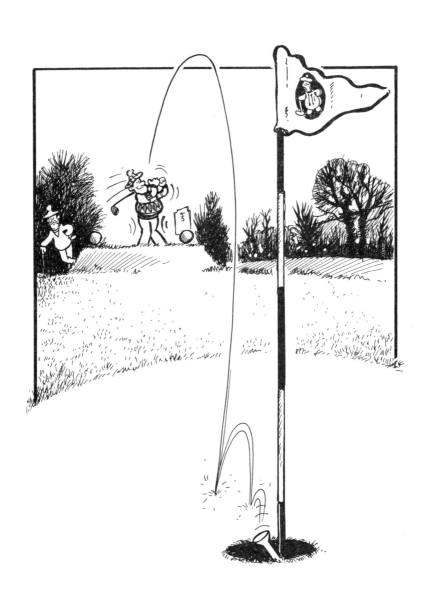

The Tee Shot.

The Successful Birdie Attempt

The Eagle...often seen
in the Scottish Highlands.

The Albatross....
once achieved, never forgotten.

Stone dead

The Golf Widow.

Head to Head Matchplay.

The Common Grip

and the **Interlocking Grip**

Chip & Run Shot

The Duck Hook

not to be confused with the
Water Hazard.

Winter rules permit a player to improve his lie
whilst on the fairway, without incurring a
penalty shot....**The Preferred Lie**

The Texas Wedge

The Slice

The Short Iron

The Banana Shot

and last but not least
The Swing